1/02
DUD

DK DORLING KINDERSLEY *READERS*

Level 2

Dinosaur Dinners
Fire Fighter!
Bugs! Bugs! Bugs!
Slinky, Scaly Snakes!
Animal Hospital
The Little Ballerina
Munching, Crunching, Sniffing
    and Snooping
The Secret Life of Trees
Winking, Blinking, Wiggling
    and Waggling

Astronaut: Living in Space
Twisters!
Holiday! Celebration Days
    around the World
The Story of Pocahontas
Horse Show
Survivors: The Night the Titanic Sank
Eruption! The Story of Volcanoes
LEGO: Castle Under Attack!
LEGO: Rocket Rescue

Level 3

Spacebusters
Beastly Tales
Shark Attack!
Titanic
Invaders from Outer Space
Movie Magic
Plants Bite Back!
Time Traveler
Bermuda Triangle
Tiger Tales
Aladdin
Heidi
Zeppelin: The Age of the Airship

Spies
Terror on the Amazon
Disasters at Sea
The Story of Anne Frank
Abraham Lincoln: Lawyer, Leader,
    Legend
George Washington: Soldier, Hero,
    President
LEGO: Mission to the Arctic
NFL: Troy Aikman
NFL: Super Bowl Heroes
MLB: Home Run Heroes
MLB: Roberto Clemente

Level 4

Days of the Knights
Volcanoes
Secrets of the Mummies
Pirates!
Horse Heroes
Trojan Horse
Micromonsters
Going for Gold!
Extreme Machines
Flying Ace: The Story of Amelia Earhart
Robin Hood
Black Beauty
Free at Last! The Story of
    Martin Luther King, Jr.
Joan of Arc
Spooky Spinechillers
Welcome to The Globe! The
    Story of Shakespeare's Theater
Antarctic Adventure

Space Station
Atlantis
Dinosaur Detectives
Danger on the Mountain: Scaling
    the World's Highest Peaks
LEGO: Race for Survival
NFL: NFL's Greatest Upsets
NFL: Terrell Davis
WCW: Going for Goldberg
WCW: Sting in the Tail
WCW: Fit for the Title
WCW: Finishing Moves
MLB: Strikeout Kings
MLB: Super Shortstops: Jeter,
    Nomar, and A-Rod
The Story of the X-Men: How It
    All Began
Creating the X-Men: How Comic
    Books Come to Life

A Note to Parents

Dorling Kindersley Readers is a compelling new program for beginning readers, designed in conjunction with leading literacy experts, including Dr. Linda Gambrell, President of the National Reading Conference and past board member of the International Reading Association.

Beautiful illustrations and superb full-color photographs combine with engaging, easy-to-read stories to offer a fresh approach to each subject in the series. Each *Dorling Kindersley Reader* is guaranteed to capture a child's interest while developing his or her reading skills, general knowledge, and love of reading.

The four levels of *Dorling Kindersley Readers* are aimed at different reading abilities, enabling you to choose the books that are exactly right for your child:

Level 1 – Beginning to read
Level 2 – Beginning to read alone
Level 3 – Reading alone
Level 4 – Proficient readers

The "normal" age at which a child begins to read can be anywhere from three to eight years old, so these levels are intended only as a general guideline.

No matter which level you select, you can be sure that you are helping your child learn to read, then read to learn!

Dorling DK Kindersley

LONDON, NEW YORK, SYDNEY, DELHI, PARIS,
MUNICH, and JOHANNESBURG

A DORLING KINDERSLEY BOOK
www.dk.com

Produced by Southern Lights
Custom Publishing

For Dorling Kindersley
Publisher Andrew Berkhut
Executive Editor Andrea Curley
Art Director Tina Vaughan
Illustrator Ernie Eldredge

Reading Consultant
Linda B. Gambrell, Ph.D.

First American Edition, 2001
00 01 02 03 04 05 10 9 8 7 6 5 4 3 2 1
Published in the United States by
Dorling Kindersley Publishing, Inc.
95 Madison Avenue, New York, New York 10016

Published in Great Britain by Dorling Kindersley Limited.

Library of Congress Cataloging-in-Publication Data

Fontes, Justine.
   George Washington: soldier, hero, president / by Justine and Ron
Fontes.–1st American ed.
   p.cm.–(Dorling Kindersley readers)
   ISBN 0-7894-7378-X – ISBN 0-7894-7377-1 (pbk)
   1. Washington, George, 1732-1799–Juvenile literature. 2.
Presidents–United States–Biography–Juvenile literature. [1.
Washington, George, 1732-1799. 2. Presidents.] I. Fontes, Ron. II.
Title. III. Series.

E312.66. K66 2001
973.4'1'092–dc21
[B]   00-055539

Printed and bound in China by L. Rex Printing Co., Ltd.

The publisher would like to thank the following for their
kind permission to reproduce their photographs and illustrations:
Key: t=top; b=below; l=left; r=right; c=center
The American Revolution: A Picture Sourcebook, Dover Publications,
Inc.: 22t, 24b, 26-27b, 32, 40b; Bettman/CORBIS: 6b, 13b, 20t, 23b,
24t, 34b, 41b, 42c, 47; DK Picture Library: 9r, 15br, 28b; Library of
Congress: 19, 25, 27r, 29; The Mariners' Museum, Newport News, VA:
12; Mount Vernon Ladies' Association: 7, 15bl, 36, 38b, 39t;
National Museums of Scotland: 9bl

see our complete catalog at
www.dk.com

Contents

George Washington

Soldier, Hero, President

Written by Justine & Ron Fontes

DK
A Dorling Kindersley Book

Student and surveyor

Virginia once had more wild animals than people and many more trees than buildings. Most of America belonged to the Native Americans. European nations like England and France ruled small colonies and wanted to rule the rest of the land.

Colonies for Power and Profit

From 1500-1800, European countries sent settlers all over the world to live in colonies. These new lands provided the mother country with valuables like gold and spices or, in the case of America, crops like cotton and tobacco.

England owned the 13 American colonies, including Virginia. The people in the colonies were ruled by English governors and were subjects of the English king.

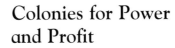

King George III

Much of Virginia was not yet mapped when George Washington's father bought land for a big farm called a plantation. George was born there on February 11, 1732, and was followed by 5 brothers and sisters. He liked to fish, swim, and ride horses.

5

There were no schools near George's home; he learned reading, writing, and arithmetic at home from a tutor. Tutors were traveling teachers.

George never learned to spell well. But he was great at math. His father planned to send George to school in England when he was old enough.

Honestly, George!

A famous story claims George cut down a cherry tree when he was a boy. His angry father asked, "Who chopped down that tree?" And even though he knew he would get in trouble, George said, "I did, Father. I cannot tell a lie."

The story was probably made up, but it is a true picture of George's character. George was very honest all his life.

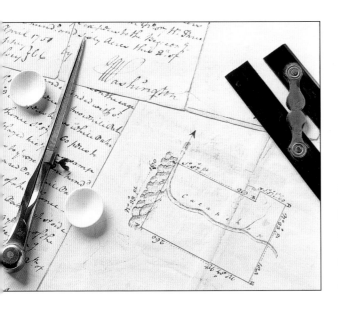

George's father used surveying tools and math to measure the land he bought.

But when George was 11, his father suddenly died. Instead of going to school in England, George stayed home to help his mother run the farm and take care of his younger brothers and sisters. He grew up fast.

One day, while cleaning up, George found his father's surveying tools. He decided to learn to survey, too. He practiced on a turnip field and a pine forest. Being good at math helped.

George missed his father, but he still
had someone to look up to—his half-
brother, Lawrence, who was 14 years
older. Lawrence had gone to school in
England and was a colonial officer in
the British Army. He fought for the
English in the Caribbean War.

After the war, Lawrence came back to America to run his own plantation, called Mount Vernon. George went to live there with Lawrence and his wife when he was 15 years old.

When Lawrence's soldier friends visited, George listened to their talk about moving troops and supplying them with food and weapons. He learned a lot about military strategy and how to fight with a sword.

A fencing foil is a thin sword.
Fencing is fighting with a sword.
George, being tall and athletic,
learned to fence very well.

George also kept up with his surveying. When he was only 16, he was hired by a rich farmer to survey his lands.

George had a great time on his first trip away from home. He climbed mountains and slept on straw in huts or outside under the stars.

In the wilds of Virginia, George met tough frontiersmen and watched Native American dances. He wore Indian clothes and learned native woodcraft. The Indians showed George how to move silently through the woods.

George did a good job mapping the land. The next year, he became Surveyor of Culpepper County, Virginia.

George was only 17! But people trusted George because he was so tall, honest, and responsible.

In George's time, a trip to the Caribbean meant a 5-week sea voyage.

George bought land with the money he earned. He also helped Lawrence run Mount Vernon.

Lawrence had been sick ever since the Caribbean War. He thought a warmer climate might help. He and

George went to the island of Barbados in the Caribbean Sea.

Sadly, the trip didn't help Lawrence. And George caught smallpox!

Smallpox was a serious disease that killed many people and left others with terrible scars.

Lawrence died soon after he sent George home. At age 20, George became the master of Mount Vernon.

Smallpox was a highly contagious (easy-to-catch) disease similar to chicken pox, only much worse. The symptoms were like flu, but with itchy blisters that often left deep scars. Until recently there was no treatment for smallpox, which killed 40% of the people who caught it and left others blind or hurt in other ways.

Soldier

George also took over Lawrence's rank in the Virginia Army. In 1753, the governor sent George on a dangerous mission. George had to take a letter to Fort LeBoeuf, a French fort in Ohio. The letter demanded that France leave its forts in the Ohio Valley.

Both England and France wanted America. The French claimed a lot of land in North America, from Canada to Louisiana. They built forts in an attempt to claim all the land to the west.

George and his men trekked through rough wilderness full of hostile Indians. Some tribes liked the French, some liked the English. Many hated all white intruders. But some Seneca warriors agreed to help George reach Fort LeBeouf.

Winter was in full force, making the trip home from Fort LeBeouf even harder.

The French commander read the governor's letter—and said no! Neither France nor the Indians would give up America without a fight!

Night Writer

The governor was impressed with George's determination to deliver his letter and its reply. But instead of rewarding him with a warm bed, the governor demanded a report for a meeting the next morning. George stayed up all night writing by candlelight. The report was later published, and read by the English king and Parliament.

George's mission marked the start of the French and Indian War. The French and Indians were fighting together against the English.

In 1755, the English sent Major General Braddock, a highly respected and experienced officer, to America to protect their colonies. George was eager to learn from such a great soldier. But Braddock could only fight the English way. His soldiers wore bright red coats.

They marched in neat lines, in time to loud fife music and drums.

George and other colonial officers tried to warn Braddock that war was different in America. Braddock refused to change. He was killed, along with many of his soldiers. George led the survivors home. He learned that a truly great leader must always learn—or die.

Farmer, friend, and statesman

For his brave deeds, George was made Commander of the Virginia Militia. A militia is a volunteer army. His job was impossible: to defend 350 miles of frontier without enough soldiers or supplies.

On a rare break from battle, George dined at a friend's house. There he met Martha Custis and her two children.

George said she made him feel instantly at home. The next day, George asked Martha to marry him as soon as he could leave the army. And she did.

George nicknamed Martha's children Patsy and Jacky. They all lived at Mount Vernon.

George rode his big horse all over Mount Vernon, checking on plants,

Mount Vernon

George and Martha's plantation produced a variety of crops including tobacco, potatoes, wheat, rye, and barley. He also bred dogs, cattle, and some of the finest horses in Virginia. The plantation was almost a village itself, with a weaving house, dairy, wash house, smoke house, blacksmiths, cobblers, brickmakers, and other craftsmen.

trees, and animals. He experimented with different soils and crops. Soon, Mount Vernon was one of the best plantations in the colony!

George also became a member of the Virginia State Legislature, which helped make laws for the colony.

The Boston Tea Party

Some Americans got tired of paying taxes to England without having a voice in how the money would be spent. They protested against "taxation without representation" by refusing to buy English goods, like tea. During the Boston Tea Party 50 angry Americans disguised as Mohawk Indians dumped 340 chests of English tea in the sea!

George realized America had problems. To pay for the French and Indian War, England put high taxes on imported goods.

George proposed that Americans refuse to buy things from England. This protest sent a clear message to England that the colonies would not put up with unfair taxes. It had another good effect. Americans bought American products—so colonial industries grew!

However, the situation in the colonies got worse. England came up with new taxes. When the Americans protested, England sent troops.

The Americans got together to decide what to do. Leaders and thinkers from each colony formed the Continental Congress.

They decided America needed an army to fight the English. They voted for George to be Commander-in-Chief of the new Continental Army. He agreed, but refused any pay. George wanted only to do his duty.

General

On July 3, 1775, George took command. He was very disappointed. The men of the Continental Army were not professional soldiers. They were farmers, backwoodsmen, clerks, dockworkers, cobblers, and fishermen.

They were not used to marching or following orders. They did not have enough uniforms, guns, bullets, or food.

In the fall of 1775, smallpox swept through the Continental Army. Thousands of men got sick. George was immune to smallpox because he had had the disease when he was 19.

Instead of going home to visit Martha that winter, George stayed to encourage his ailing army.

Minutemen

The American colonial fighters were called Minutemen. Professional soldiers waited in a fort for orders to fight. Minutemen came from the countryside "in a minute." George sadly observed that they also disappeared in a minute when it was time to drill! Minutemen were more independent than professional soldiers, but they had great fighting spirit.

Meanwhile, the American colonies were slowly becoming a nation. In January 1776, America got its first flag: 13 red and white stripes, which stood for the 13 colonies.

On July 4, 1776, the colonies officially became a country when the Continental Congress signed the Declaration of Independence.

Public reading of the Declaration of Independence.

George read the thrilling document to his troops. It said America was no longer a group of colonies under English rule, but one nation free to rule itself. The American Revolution had begun!

The Declaration of Independence

A declaration is a formal statement. Thomas Jefferson was the chief writer of the Declaration of Independence. He had help from a committee that included John Adams and Benjamin Franklin, among others. They spent a month writing and rewriting the one-page Declaration before Congress signed it. Americans celebrate Independence Day on July 4 in honor of this historic occasion.

However, declaring independence wasn't enough. England refused to give up the colonies without a fight.

Rich, powerful England had a fleet of war ships and lots of well-trained troops with plenty of uniforms, weapons, and supplies. They also hired mercenaries (professional soldiers) from Germany. The Americans called these tough soldiers "Hessians."

The English fleet lands troops in Boston.

Against all this, the Americans had little more than the will to win. George suffered a series of defeats. The best he could do was get his troops away before too many were killed.

George did this brilliantly. But he was getting tired of defeats and retreats!

Uniform of a Hessian soldier.

In the winter of 1776, the English stopped fighting. Wars always stopped in winter. After all, who would be crazy enough to battle ice and snow as well as the enemy?

The English war ships left. Most of their army went home. About 1,500 Hessians were camped at Trenton, New Jersey. The American army was just across the Delaware River. The Hessians celebrated Christmas with plenty of wine.

On the cold night of December 26, 1776, George decided his army needed

Wet weather

The weather was so bad, the Americans could not use their guns. The gunpowder was too soggy to fire! So they put bayonets (removable knives) on the ends of their rifles.

a party of its own—a surprise party! George got the fishermen among his troops to do what they did best. They quietly rowed back and forth all night, through sleet and rain, carrying the Americans across the icy river.

The Americans would have been easy targets if the Hessians had spotted them. But George's daring plan worked!

At 8:00 in the morning, George and his troops attacked. The sleepy Hessians were completely surprised!

In 45 minutes, George and his troops had captured 900 mercenaries — and lost only four men.

After George's victory at Trenton, England sent more troops to New Jersey. They were sure they could defeat the rebels with all those new soldiers.

But George played another trick. This time his army built big campfires. The English thought the colonial

soldiers were warming their feet. But
they were really slipping silently into
the woods.

George showed them how to move
quietly like the Indians had taught him.

By morning, the Americans were
miles away from their camp. George's
second surprise attack on the English
post in Princeton won another victory!

Suddenly, the ragged army of rebels looked able to beat the mighty British Empire! To celebrate the victories and

To make his troops look like a unified army, George had them put sprigs of greenery in their caps. They marched by fours, making the parade seem longer.

Ring in Freedom

The Continental Congress had met at Independence Hall in Philadelphia to draft the Declaration of Independence. The bell that hung there became known as the Liberty Bell because it rang on July 4, 1776, to proclaim America's independence.

rally support for the Continental Army, George led a parade of troops through Philadelphia, the capital of the new nation.

The rows of continental soldiers wore a shabby assortment of tattered uniforms, work clothes, Indian shirts, and even some enemy coats. The men sang and drummed loudly to show their fighting spirit.

Beloved leader

More than hope was needed to win the Revolutionary War. The Continental Army continued to suffer defeats and retreats. In December 1777, the British marched into Philadelphia! Congress fled, and the English settled down for a comfortable winter in America's capital.

Meanwhile, George and his men

made their weary way to a nearby place called Valley Forge. Many soldiers didn't have shoes. They wrapped their frozen feet with rags. But ice cut through the rags, and the men left a bloody trail in the snow.

George had soldiers chop down trees and build log huts. He stayed in a tent until the hut city was finished.

Now the army had shelter but not enough food, clothing, blankets, medicine, or doctors. During that terrible winter, 2,500 Americans died from cold, hunger, and disease. Another 2,500 sneaked home.

But the 6,000 who stayed became as tough and stubborn as their leader. George refused to give up the fight for America. And help was on the way!

A long-time enemy of England,
France liked the American ideals of
freedom and fair government. So the
French decided to help the Americans.

First, France sent a military expert to train the Continental troops. Baron Von Steuben was shocked by the frozen, starved American soldiers but was impressed by their spirit. He drilled the men from sunrise to sunset and turned them into real soldiers.

In 1778, France sent money and troops. After three years of fighting, the British asked for peace talks. Then, in 1783, the talks finally ended and the war was officially over. The Americans had won their independence!

George modestly gave credit for the victory to "every Officer and Soldier in the combined Army in this Occasion." But the truth is, without George, America might never have won.

The most famous and beloved hero in the new nation just wanted to go home. The gray-haired, 51-year-old had lost most of his teeth due to the bad army diet. Writing by candlelight had strained his eyes. But George was happy to be back at Mount Vernon.

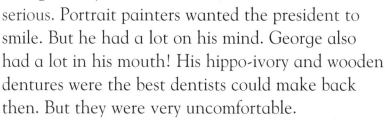

Tooth Trouble

When he was older, George always looked serious. Portrait painters wanted the president to smile. But he had a lot on his mind. George also had a lot in his mouth! His hippo-ivory and wooden dentures were the best dentists could make back then. But they were very uncomfortable.

In May 1787, state representatives decided to write a constitution to describe how the new American government should work. The delegates voted for George to lead the group.

Though he was old and tired, George took the job. He spent a long, hot summer in Philadelphia listening to delegates argue. George did his best to make sure the powers of the new government were clear.

In June 1788, the Constitution was approved by most of the states. Now America had a real government.

President

On April 6, 1789, George was unanimously elected to be the first president of the United States.

America's capital had moved from Philadelphia to New York City. The new president had to travel to the new capital to be sworn in. George expected a quick, quiet journey from Mount Vernon to New York. Instead, parades, parties, and cheering crowds greeted him in every town! The parade in Trenton was very special.

At the New Jersey shore, George boarded a special barge to cross the Hudson River. Thirteen ships' captains rowed the beautiful barge to New York City. The harbor was filled with other boats draped in red, white, and blue.

That night, the town blazed with
bonfires and brilliant fireworks—all
to salute George!

The Trenton parade was like an ancient Roman triumph.
The arch was supported by 13 columns entwined with
evergreen. Girls tossed flowers at his feet.

George tried to be a fair president. There were two different parties, or groups, in the country. One favored a strong central government, run by the

Tell it like it is

Americans are free to say whatever they want, and can even criticize their own government in cartoons published in newspapers. The right of free speech, and free press, among other things, are granted in the Bill of Rights. The Bill of Rights contains the first amendments to the Constitution. (An amendment is an addition or change.)

people with the most property. The other believed in states' rights and the rights of working people.

George worked with men from both parties. He also tried to balance the needs of all the states.

George toured the tiny nation, listening to people's problems. He welcomed all Americans to come and talk to him.

George supported the Bill of Rights. He had fought hard for America's freedom. The Bill of Rights makes sure that the government won't take away freedom.

In 1792, George was once again unanimously elected president. His second term was even harder than the first term!

In 1793, war broke out between England and France. The French reminded George of the help they'd given the American Revolution. They wanted America to help France.

George did not think the new country was strong enough to fight so soon. Despite critics, George did what he thought was best for America and stayed out of the war.

He also signed peace treaties with the Indians and Spain.

Many people expected George to be president for the rest of his life, like a king. But George refused to run for a third term.

He believed the American government would be better off with a new leader every four to eight years.

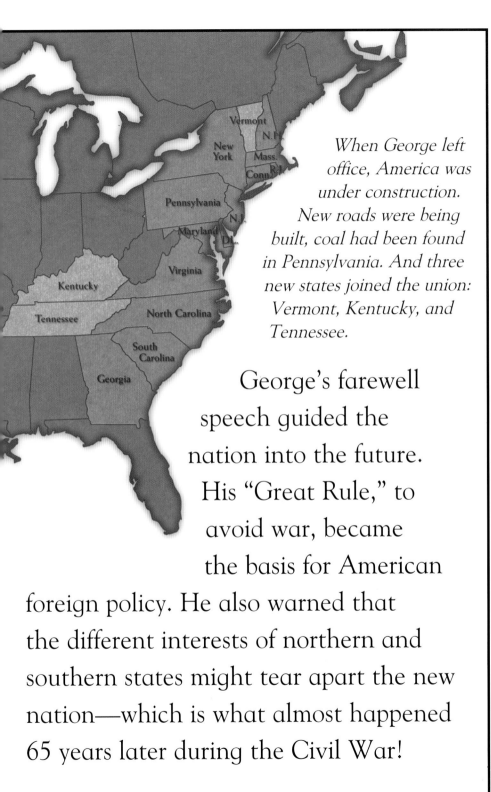

When George left office, America was under construction. New roads were being built, coal had been found in Pennsylvania. And three new states joined the union: Vermont, Kentucky, and Tennessee.

George's farewell speech guided the nation into the future. His "Great Rule," to avoid war, became the basis for American foreign policy. He also warned that the different interests of northern and southern states might tear apart the new nation—which is what almost happened 65 years later during the Civil War!

George and Martha were very happy to return to Mount Vernon. Every morning, George rode his horse to inspect his beloved trees and fields. Sometimes the energetic 67-year-old rode 15 miles north to watch the building of the new capital city, named Washington in his honor.

One windy, wet, and miserable morning, George caught a bad cold. Doctors treated him with bleeding cups, which allowed them to remove blood.

Back then, doctors thought blood carried disease. We now know that blood also keeps people strong. Within two days, on December 14, 1799, George was dead.

As a surveyor, George Washington measured and marked the land. As a farmer, he nurtured it. As a soldier, he fought for it. As a president, he guided it. As a legend, he still inspires it.

On February 21, 1885, crowds gathered in Washington to see the new monument honoring the Father of the Nation. The tall spike reached up toward heaven, like the ideals of the hero who loved America.

Glossary

Capital
The city that houses a country's government. Washington, D.C., is the capital of the United States.

Colony
A group of people who settle in a distant land that is ruled by their native country. The American colonies were ruled by England until the Revolutionary War.

Congress
A group of representatives who gather together to decide on matters of government, like laws.

Constitution
A written statement of the laws and ideals of a country that is used as the basis of its government.

Declaration of Independence
The formal statement adopted July 4, 1776, declaring that the 13 American colonies were free and independent of England.

Delegate
A person given the right to act or vote for others; a representative of the people within his neighborhood, county, or state.

Empire
A state uniting many territories and peoples under one ruler. Before the Revolutionary War, the British Empire included America.

Hessians
The name Americans gave to the German soldiers hired by England to fight in the Revolutionary War.

Immune
Protected from something harmful, such as a disease. People who have had smallpox (or chicken-pox) are immune to future infection.

Legislature
A group of people given the power to make laws.

Mercenary
A soldier who fights for pay, not for patriotism (love of country).

Militia
An army composed of citizens (ordinary people) rather than professional soldiers.

Minutemen
The members of the American militia who volunteered to be ready "in a minute" to fight for their country.

Mount Vernon
George Washington's home in Virginia. The mansion has been restored to look the way it did in Washington's day and is open to tourists.

Plantation
A large farm.

Surveyor
Someone who measures land to establish boundaries.

Term
A period of time with definite limits. A U.S. president's term of office is 4 years with a limit of two terms.

Unanimous
Agreeing completely. In a unanimous election one candidate gets all the votes.

Index